The book of five rings

MIYAMOTO Musashi

CONTENTS

INTRODUCTION

For many years, I have dedicated myself to learning the Way of Strategy, known as Ni Ten Ichi Ryu, and I have decided to present it in writing for the first time. We are currently in the first ten days of the tenth month of the twentieth year of Kanei (1645). I have climbed Mount Iwato in the Higo region of Kyushu to pay homage to the heavens, pray to Kwannon, and prostrate before Buddha. I am a warrior from the province of Harima, Shinmen Musashi No Kami Fujiwara No Genshin, and I am sixty years old.

Since my youth, I have been drawn to the Way of Strategy. My first duel took place at thirteen, and I defeated a warrior of the Shinto school, Arima Kihei. At sixteen, I beat a skilled warrior named

Tadashima Akiyama. At twenty-one, I went to the capital and faced many warriors, winning every duel.

Subsequently, I traveled from province to province, challenging warriors from different schools, and I have never lost, even after about sixty encounters. This happened between the ages of thirteen and twenty-nine. At thirty, reflecting on my past, I realized that my victories were not the result of my mastery of strategy. Perhaps it was innate talent, destiny, or maybe the strategies of other schools were simply inferior. Afterwards, I studied day and night to discover the principle and understood the Way of Strategy at fifty.

Since then, I live without following any particular Way. Through the virtue of strategy, I practice many arts and skills, all self-taught. To write this book, I have not used the laws of Buddha, nor the teachings of Confucius, nor the ancient tales of war or books on martial tactics. I take up the pen to explain the true spirit of the Ichi school, as reflected in the Way of Heaven and by Kwannon. We are on the night of the tenth day of the tenth month, at the hour of the tiger (between 3 and 5 in the morning).

THE BOOK OF EARTH

Strategy is the art of the warrior. Commanders must master this art, and soldiers must know this Way. Currently, no warrior in the world truly understands the Way of Strategy.

There are various Ways. There is the Way of salvation through the law of Buddha, the Way of Confucius guiding learning, the Way of healing through medicine, teaching poetry through the Way of Waka, as well as the Ways of tea, archery, and many other arts and skills. Each practices the Way that best suits them.

It is often said that a warrior follows the dual Way of the pen and the sword, and he should familiarize himself with both aspects. Even a person without innate talent can become a warrior by dedicating themselves diligently to these two facets of the Way.

The Way of Strategy

In China and Japan, practitioners of the Way were often called 'masters of strategy'. Every warrior must learn this Way.

Recently, some have become known as strategists, but they are usually ordinary fencers. The servants of the Kashima Kantori shrines in the Hitachi province received divine teachings and created schools based on these instructions, traveling from region to region to teach. This is what 'strategy' means today.

In the past, strategy was part of the Ten Skills and Seven Arts, considered as a beneficial practice. Although it is an art, it was not limited to fencing. The true essence of fencing cannot be understood solely through the techniques of this sport.

Observe the world: the arts are commercialized. People use tools to sell themselves, making the container more important than the content. In this Way of Strategy, teachers and students are obsessed with showcasing and exhibiting their techniques, seeking to accelerate the recognition of their talent. They talk about 'this dojo' or 'that dojo', always in search of profit. As someone once said, 'An immature strategy is a source of sorrow'. This statement was accurate.

There are four ways to live one's life: as a gentleman, farmer, artisan, or merchant.

The Way of the farmer involves using farming tools, observing the seasons from spring to autumn.

The Way of the merchant is different: for example, a wine maker procures ingredients to earn a living. The merchant always aims to make a profit.

Then there is the Way of the gentleman warrior, mastering the art of wielding his weapons. He must understand and appreciate the virtue of his armament. Without a taste for strategy, can he really perceive the value of the art of war?

Finally, the Way of the artisan, like that of the carpenter, requires mastering the use of tools and planning meticulously before executing his work.

These four Ways represent the paths of life of the gentleman, farmer, artisan, and merchant.

Comparing the Way of the Carpenter to Strategy

The comparison with carpentry is made through the link to house construction. Whether it's noble houses, warrior residences, the Four Houses, the ruin or prosperity of homes, the style, tradition, or name of the house, the carpenter follows a master construction plan, much like the strategist with his campaign plan. To master the art of war, meditate on this book. The master is to the needle what the student is to the thread: constant practice is necessary.

Just like the chief carpenter, the commander must know the natural rules, those of the country, and those of the houses. The chief carpenter must understand the architectural theory of towers and temples, the plans of palaces, and organize his team to build houses. The Way of the carpenter and that of the commander are identical.

In construction, the choice of wood is crucial. Straight and knot-free wood is used for visible pillars, while slightly flawed wood is used for interior pillars. The most beautiful wood, even if a bit fragile, is used for thresholds, doors, etc. Strong wood, even if knotty, can be judiciously used in construction. Weak or excessively knotty wood is used for scaffolding, then as firewood.

The chief carpenter assigns tasks according to the skills of each: some lay floors, make sliding doors, thresholds; others, less skilled, make wedges or other various works. If the chief knows his workers well and employs them appropriately, the result will be satisfactory. He must know the strengths and weaknesses of his team, move among them without demanding the impossible, understand their morale and spirit, and encourage them as needed. This aligns with the principle of strategy.

The Way of Strategy

Just like a soldier, the carpenter sharpens his own tools. He carries his equipment in his toolbox and works under the orders of his team leader. With his axe, he shapes columns and beams, forms floors and shelves with a plane, performs precise cuts and carvings, bringing a finish as excellent as his skills allow. Such is the practice of carpenters. When a carpenter masters his craft and understands the measurements, he can become a team leader.

The carpenter's goal is to have sharp tools to create miniature shrines, writing shelves, tables, paper lanterns, cutting boards, and pot lids. These are the specialties of the carpenter. Things are similar for the soldier. It would be beneficial for you to meditate deeply on this.

The carpenter's achievement is seen in work without deformations, with aligned joints, a properly planed piece that fits well, not just finished by sections. This is essential.

If you wish to understand this Way, consider deeply each element stated in this book, one by one. Thorough examination is necessary.

Outline of the Five Books of this Strategy Manual

The Way is presented in five books, each addressing a different aspect: Earth (the foundation), Water, Fire, Wind (tradition), and Void (the illusory nature of earthly things).

The 'Earth' book explains the essence of the Way of Strategy from the perspective of my Ichi method. It is complicated to understand the true Way only through fencing. One must know the smallest and the largest things, the most superficial and the most profound. The 'Earth' book is the starting point, like a straight road drawn on the ground.

The second book is 'Water.' With water as the base, the spirit becomes as fluid as it. Water takes the shape of its container, it can be a stream or a raging ocean. The 'Water' book clarifies the elements of the Ichi school.

By mastering the principles of fencing, defeating one man means being able to defeat anyone. The principle is the same, whether facing one or ten million men. The strategist transforms the small into large, like a large Buddha conceived from a small model.

The third book is 'Fire.' This book deals with combat, where the spirit of fire is fierce, regardless of the size of the battle. Whether in duels or massive battles, the spirit can expand or shrink.

The fourth book, 'Wind,' is not about my Ichi school but about other schools of strategy. By 'Wind,' I refer to the old, the current, and the family traditions of strategy, thus explaining the global strategies. Knowing others is essential for knowing oneself.

Finally, the fifth book is that of the 'Void.' By 'Void,' I mean that which has neither beginning nor end. Reaching this principle means not reaching the principle. The Way of strategy is the Way of nature. By understanding the power of nature and the rhythm of any situation, you can naturally strike and counter-strike. All this constitutes the Way of the Void, and in this book, I intend to show how to follow the true Way in harmony with nature.

Ichi Ryu Ni To (One School - Two Swords)

Warriors, whether they are commanders or soldiers, carry two swords at their belt. In the past, these weapons were called the long sword and the sword. Today, they are referred to as the sword and the companion sword. Simply put, in our culture, the warrior carries two swords, it is the Way of the warrior.

'Nito Ichi Ryu' demonstrates the advantages of wielding these two swords simultaneously.

The spear and the halberd are outdoor weapons. Students of the Ichi school should train from the beginning with both the long sword and the standard sword, in either hand. A truth: when you risk your life, you must fully exploit your weapons. It would be wrong not to do so and to die leaving a sword in its sheath.

Holding a sword with two hands limits freedom of movement.

Therefore, my method recommends holding the sword with one hand. This principle does not apply to more cumbersome weapons like the spear or halberd, but swords can be wielded with one hand. This is also more practical on horseback, on uneven, swampy, muddy, rocky terrain, or in a crowd. However, if an enemy is difficult to defeat with one hand, use both. With training, wielding a sword with one hand will become less difficult. Everything is complicated at the beginning. With practice, one becomes stronger and more skillful.

As explained in the second book, the Book of Water, there is no quick method to wield the long sword. The long sword must be wielded broadly, and the companion sword more restrictively. This is the first principle to understand.

According to the Ichi school, whether the weapon is long or short, you can win. In short, the Way of the Ichi school is the spirit of victory, regardless of the weapon and its size.

In a fight against multiple opponents, it is better to use two swords, especially if you want to capture a prisoner.

It is impossible to explain everything in detail. From one element, learn ten thousand. Once you master the Way of Strategy, nothing will escape you. Study diligently.

The Advantage of the Two Japanese Characters Meaning 'Strategy'

Experts in the long sword are referred to as strategists. In other military arts, those who master the bow are called archers, specialists in the spear are spear throwers, those who excel with firearms are sharpshooters, and masters of the halberd are halberdiers. However, we do not call masters of the long sword 'swordsmen', nor do we speak of 'specialists in the companion sword'. Bows, firearms, spears, and halberds are all equipment of warriors, and are undoubtedly part of strategy. Mastering the long sword allows one to govern oneself and the world, making this

11

sword the foundation of strategy. The principle is: 'strategy by means of the long sword'.

If a man achieves mastery of the long sword, he can defeat ten opponents. As one man can defeat ten, a hundred men can defeat a thousand, and a thousand can defeat ten thousand. In my strategy, one man is equivalent to ten thousand, making this strategy the complete art of the warrior.

The Way of the warrior does not include other ways, such as Confucianism, Buddhism, certain traditions, arts, and dance. However, deeply knowing the Way allows one to recognize it in all things. Everyone must perfect their specific Way.

The Advantage of Weapons in Strategy

Each weapon has its appropriate time and place for use.

The companion sword is ideal in a confined space or for close combat. As for the long sword, it proves effective in all situations.

On the battlefield, the halberd is less efficient than the spear. The spear allows for taking the initiative, while the halberd is more defensive. In the hands of two equally skilled individuals, the spear offers a slight advantage. Although the spear and halberd each have their uses, they are limited in confined spaces and are not suitable for capturing a prisoner. They are primarily open-field weapons.

If you focus solely on techniques for confined spaces, your vision will be narrow and you will lose sight of the true Way, which will be detrimental in real confrontations.

The bow is a tactical asset at the beginning of a battle, especially on open terrains, allowing for rapid firing from a formation of spearmen. However, it is not ideal during sieges or when the enemy is more than forty yards away. This is why there are few traditional schools of archery today.

The rifle is unmatched for defending a fortification. It is supreme on the battlefield before hand-to-hand combat, but becomes useless once swords are drawn. An advantage of the bow is the visibility of its arrows in flight, allowing for adjusting aim, something the rifle does not allow.

Weapons, like horses, must be sturdy and flawless. Horses must have a sure gait, swords must cut effectively, and spears and halberds must withstand intense use. Bows and rifles must be robust, and the aesthetics of weapons must give way to functionality.

Avoid becoming attached to any particular weapon. Too much familiarity with a weapon is as detrimental as not knowing it sufficiently. Do not merely imitate others: choose weapons you can handle with ease. It is counterproductive for commanders and soldiers to have preferences in weapons. These are aspects to master perfectly.

Timing in Strategy

Timing is crucial in all things, and mastering it in strategy requires much practice.

Timing is essential in dance and music, which cannot be rhythmic without appropriate timing. It also plays a role in the military arts, archery, firearms shooting, and horseback riding. Each skill and ability involves a sense of timing.

Timing is also present in the Void.

Timing rhythms the entire life of the warrior, in his moments of success and failure, harmony and discord. Similarly, in the way of the merchant, timing affects the rise and fall of capital. Every phenomenon obeys a timing of ascent and decline, which you must be able to discern. In strategy, several temporal considerations must be taken into account. From the outset, you must distinguish between applicable timing and that which is not, and identify the relevant timing among large and small events, fast and slow timings, first observing the distance and the context. This is fundamental in strategy. Knowing the timing of the context is crucial, otherwise your strategy will be uncertain.

You win battles with the timing of the Void, derived from the timing of deception, by knowing the timing of the enemy and using a timing he does not expect.

The five books deal mainly with timing. You must train intensively to understand this.

If you practice day and night according to the strategy of the Ichi school, your mind will naturally broaden. This is how large-scale strategy and close-combat strategy spread throughout the world. For the first time, this is recorded in the five books: Earth, Water, Fire, Tradition (Wind), and Void.

For those who wish to learn my strategy, here is the way:

Do not think dishonestly.

The Way is in training.

Become acquainted with every art.

Understand the ways of all professions.

Discern the gain and loss in worldly matters.

Develop intuitive judgment and understanding of everything.

Perceive what is invisible.

Pay attention to the details.

Do not act unnecessarily.

Start by embedding these fundamental principles in your heart and train in the Way of Strategy. Without a large-scale vision, it will be difficult for you to master strategy. With the learning and mastery of this strategy, you will never lose, even against twenty or thirty enemies. Above all, you must dedicate yourself to strategy and adhere seriously to the Way. You will be able to defeat opponents in real fights and triumph through your gaze. With enough training, you can defeat ten men with your spirit. Is not reaching this level synonymous with invincibility?

Furthermore, in large-scale strategy, a superior man will skillfully manage many subordinates, behave correctly, govern the country, and take care of the people, thus preserving the ruler's discipline. If there is a Way imbued with the spirit of invincibility, allowing one to help oneself and acquire honor, it is indeed the Way of Strategy.

THE BOOK OF WATER

The spirit of the Ni Ten Ichi school of strategy finds its source in water. The Book of Water aims to explain the methods of victory, as embodied by the form of the long sword unique to the Ichi school. Language finds its limits when it comes to explaining the Way in detail, but it can be grasped intuitively. Study this book: read a word, then reflect on it. A too liberal interpretation of the meaning will lead you away from the Way.

The principles of strategy, as expressed here, are formulated in the context of single combat. However, it is essential to think comprehensively in order to acquire an understanding applicable to battles involving thousands of fighters on each side.

Strategy is distinguished in this from other disciplines: a small misunderstanding of the Way can quickly lead to confusion and the adoption of erroneous practices.

Simply reading this book will not suffice to make you reach the Way of Strategy. You must fully assimilate the content of these pages. Do not be content with reading, memorizing, or imitating: work diligently to incorporate these principles within yourself, so that you can realize the Way from your own heart.

Spiritual Maintenance in Strategy

In a strategic approach, your spiritual posture should not diverge from your normal state. In combat as in daily life, display serene determination. Face each situation without excessive tension, but also not with carelessness: your mind should be stable but without prejudice. Even in calmness, your body should not slump; and when your body is relaxed, your mind should not weaken.

Avoid having your mind influenced by your body and your body influenced by your mind. Do not lack energy, but do not have too much either. An overly exuberant mind is vulnerable, just as an overly low spirit is. Do not let your opponent perceive your state of mind.

Individuals who are weaker or more modest must fully understand the spirit of great personalities, and vice versa. Regardless of your status or size, do not let the reactions of your own body deceive you. With an open and unconstrained mind, consider things from a high viewpoint. You must cultivate both your wisdom and your spirit.

Perfect your wisdom: learn public justice, distinguish between good and evil, study the ways of different arts thoroughly. Once you can no longer be deceived by others, you will have achieved the wisdom of strategy.

The wisdom inherent in strategy is different from other forms of knowledge. On the battlefield, even in difficult moments, tirelessly pursue the study of the principles of strategy, in order to forge an unshakeable spirit.

The Gaze in Strategy

The gaze must be broad and far-reaching. This relates to the concept of the double gaze: 'Perception and Sight.' Perception is strong, while Sight is weaker.

In strategy, it is crucial to perceive distant elements as if they were close and to have a distanced view of things that are near. It is important in strategy to understand the enemy's sword and not be distracted by insignificant movements of his sword. This point deserves your attention. The type of gaze required is the same, whether for individual combat or large-scale strategy.

In strategy, you must be able to look on both sides without moving your eyes. This skill is not quickly acquired. Learn what is written here; use this type of gaze in everyday life and do not change it, regardless of the situation.

Holding the Long Sword

Hold the long sword with a light and floating sensation in the thumb and index finger, the middle finger neither too tight nor too loose, and the last two fingers tightly clenched. It is bad to have play in the hands.

When you grasp a sword, you must be resolved to cut the enemy.

While cutting, do not change your grip and your hands should not tremble. Whether you are pushing back, parrying, or forcing the enemy's sword down, adjust the pressure of your thumb and index finger slightly. Above all, the way you hold the sword must reflect your intention to cut the enemy.

The grip for combat and for sword testing is the same. There is no specific grip for 'cutting a man'.

In general, I do not like rigidity, whether in long swords or in hands. Rigidity equates to a dead hand. Flexibility, on the other hand, symbolizes a living hand. Keep this in mind.

Footwork

With the tips of your feet slightly suspended, walk firmly with your heels. Whether you move quickly or slowly, with large or small steps, your feet should always move as in a normal walk. I am not in favor of the three methods of walking known as 'hopping-foot', 'floating-foot', and 'fixed-step'.

The so-called 'Yin-Yang foot' is important in the Way. The 'Yin-Yang foot' does not mean to move only one foot. It involves moving your left-right and right-left feet during cutting, retreating, or parrying. You must not move preferentially on one foot.

The Five Guard Positions

The five positions are: High, Middle, Low, Right Side, and Left Side. These are the five. Although the position is divided into these five categories, they all pursue the same objective: to cut the enemy. There are no other positions than these five.

No matter which position you adopt, do not be conscious of creating it; think only of cutting.

Your position should be large or small depending on the situation. The High, Low, and Middle positions are decisive. The Right Side and Left Side positions are fluid. Use the Left Side or Right Side positions if there is an obstacle above your head or to one side. The decision to use Left or Right depends on the available space.

The essence of the Way is as follows. To understand these positions, you must deeply master the Middle position. This is the heart of the positions. In considering large-scale strategy, the Middle position is that of the commander, with the other four positions following his orders. You must understand and recognize this.

The Way of the Long Sword

Mastering the Way of the long sword means being able to handle the sword we normally carry with only two fingers. A thorough knowledge of the Way of the sword allows easy manipulation.

Trying to handle the long sword quickly leads to mistakes. To handle it well, it must be done calmly. If you try to move it quickly, as you would with a folding fan or a short sword, you will make a mistake by adopting a 'short sword strike' technique. You cannot defeat someone with a long sword using this method.

After striking downwards with the long sword, raise it directly; if the strike is lateral, return the sword following a lateral trajectory. Reset the sword in a reasonable position, always extending the elbows widely. Handle the sword with force. This is the Way of the long sword.

By learning to use the five approaches of my strategy, you will be able to handle a sword well. Constant practice is essential.

The Five Approaches

The first approach is that of the Middle Position. Confront the opponent with the tip of your sword directed at his face. When he attacks, deflect his sword to the right and 'accompany it'. Or, when he attacks, divert the tip of his sword by striking down, keep your long sword in place, and when he renews his attack, cut his arms from below. This is the first method. The five approaches are of the same order. You must train again and again with a long sword to learn them. By mastering my Way of the long sword, you can counter any attack of the enemy. There are no other positions than these five in the use of the long sword of Ni To.

For the second approach, from the High Position, cut the enemy at the very moment he attacks. If he dodges, keep your sword in place and, starting from the bottom, cut him if he tries to attack again. You can repeat this movement.

For the third approach, adopt the Low Position, anticipate an upward movement. When the enemy attacks, strike his hands from below. If, in doing so, he tries to strike your sword down, cut his upper arm horizontally with the impression of 'crossing'. This means that from the Low Position, you strike the enemy at the moment he attacks.

The fourth approach involves adopting the Left Side Position. When the enemy attacks, strike his hands from below. If he tries to strike your sword down, parry his blade and cut from the shoulder.

The fifth approach requires adopting the Right Side Position. In response to the enemy's attack, cross your sword from the bottom to the High Position and cut vertically from the top.

It is essential to know these methods well to master the Way of the long sword. If you master them, you can freely handle a heavy long sword. The details of these five approaches cannot be fully described here. Familiarize yourself with my method 'in harmony with the long sword', learn to measure time comprehensively, understand the enemy's sword, and get used to the five approaches from the beginning. In using them, you will always win, adjusting your timing and discerning the enemy's spirit. Think carefully about all this.

The Teaching of the 'No-Posture Stance'

The 'No-Posture Stance' means that it is not necessary to adopt what are called classical long sword postures.

However, postures do exist, embodied in the five ways of holding the long sword. Regardless of how you hold the sword, it should be positioned in a way that facilitates an effective cut of the enemy, depending on the situation, location, and your position relative to the enemy. From the High Stance, as your momentum decreases, you can adopt the Middle Stance; and from the Middle Stance, you can slightly raise the sword in your technique and adopt the High Stance. From the Low Stance, you can raise the sword and adopt the Middle Stance as needed. Depending on the situation, if you direct your sword from the Left or Right Side Stance towards the center, the Middle or Low Stance results.

The principle of this is called 'Existing - Non-Existing Stance'.

The primary element when you take a sword in hand is your intention to cut the enemy, by all means. Every time you parry, strike, leap, land a blow, or touch the enemy's sharp sword, you must cut him in the same movement. It is essential to reach this level. If you think only of striking, leaping, landing a blow, or touching the enemy, you will not be able to really cut him. More than anything, you must think of carrying your movement through to cut the enemy. You must study this thoroughly.

In larger-scale strategy, the stance is called 'Battle Formation'. These stances all aim to win battles. A rigid formation is bad. Study this carefully.

Striking the Enemy 'In One Timing'

'In One Timing' means, once you have engaged the enemy, to strike him as quickly and directly as possible, without moving your body or easing your mind, while you see that he is still undecided. The moment to strike before the enemy decides to retreat, break off, or strike, corresponds to this 'In One Timing'.

You must train to master this timing, so that you can strike in the blink of an eye.

The 'Two-Beat Abdominal Timing'

When you attack and the enemy retreats quickly, as soon as you see him tense up, you should feign a cut. Then, as soon as he relaxes, follow through and strike him. This is the 'Two-Beat Abdominal Timing'.

It is very difficult to achieve this by simply reading this book, but with a little instruction, you will quickly understand.

No Plan, No Thought

According to this method, when the enemy attacks and you also decide to attack, strike with your body, strike with your spirit, and strike from the Void with your hands, accelerating strongly. This represents the strike 'No Plan, No Thought'.

This is the most crucial striking method. It is frequently used. You must train diligently to understand it.

The Flowing Water Cut

The 'Flowing Water Cut' is used when you are engaged in a blade-to-blade fight with the enemy. If the enemy disengages and retreats quickly, attempt to attack with your long sword. Extend your body and your spirit and cut him as slowly as possible with your long sword, following your body like stagnant water. This technique, once mastered, ensures a precise cut. You must be able to discern the level of the enemy.

The Continuous Cut

When you attack and the enemy also attacks, and your swords clash, cut in a single action his head, hands, and legs. The 'Continuous Cut' is a technique that allows cutting in multiple places with a single movement of the long sword. This technique is frequently used and requires extensive practice to master.

The Fire and Stones Cut

The 'Fire and Stones Cut' involves cutting as strongly as possible, without raising the sword, when the blades clash. Act quickly and with force, using both hands, body, and legs. With proper training, this powerful strike can be mastered.

The Red Leaf Cut

The 'Red Leaf Cut' aims to disarm the enemy. In a fight, if the enemy is positioned in front of you with the intention to cut, strike, or parry, use the 'Fire and Stones Cut' with surprising force. By practicing this technique, disarming the enemy becomes easy.

The Body in Place of the Long Sword

This method can also be called 'the long sword in place of the body'. Generally, the body and the sword move together to cut the enemy. However, depending on the enemy's technique, you can first project yourself with your body and then cut with the sword. You must study this method well and practice the strikes.

Slicing and Slashing

Slicing and slashing are two different things. A good slice, regardless of its form, is decisive and requires a resolved spirit. Slashing, even if strong, even if the enemy dies instantly, remains a mere slash. You must understand this nuance. If you start by slashing the enemy's hands or legs, you must then slice with force. Slashing has the same spirit as touching. You must learn this well.

The Chinese Monkey Body

'The Chinese Monkey Body' involves not extending your arms excessively. The idea is to quickly approach the enemy without extending your arms, and do this before the enemy can attack. If you are determined not to extend your arms, you will maintain an effective distance, but the intention is to engage with your entire body. Once within arm's reach, it will be easy to move your body forward. Deepen your understanding of this technique.

The Body Coated with Glue and Lacquer

'The Body Coated with Glue and Lacquer' means to stick to the enemy without separating from him. As the enemy approaches, adhere firmly with your head, body, and legs. Generally, people advance their head and legs quickly, but their body remains behind. You must stick firmly to the enemy without leaving any space between your two bodies. Think carefully about this.

Striving for Height

'Striving for Height' means that, when you confront the enemy, you must fight to obtain a higher position without slumping. Stretch your legs, hips, and neck to find yourself facing him. When you think you have gained in height, attack vigorously. You must learn this technique.

Applying Stickiness

When the enemy attacks and you also respond with the long sword, you must advance with a sticky feeling and keep your sword against the enemy's when you parry his blow. The spirit of stickiness is not to strike hard, but to strike in such a way that the swords do not easily separate. It is better to approach as calmly as possible while striking the enemy's sword with this sticky sensation. It is important to understand the nuance between 'Stickiness' and 'Entanglement': stickiness is strong, entanglement is weak.

The Body Strike

'The Body Strike' involves approaching the enemy by finding an opening in his guard. The intention is to strike him with your body. Slightly turn your face and strike the enemy's chest with your left shoulder forward. Advance with the intention of pushing the enemy back, striking as hard as possible in sync with your breathing. With this method, you can push the enemy several meters away. You can continue to strike him until he is incapacitated. Train well.

Three Ways to Parry an Attack

There are three methods to parry an attack:

Deflect the attack to your right: When the opponent attacks, deflect his long sword towards your right, as if you were aiming at his eyes.

Parry aiming at the enemy's right eye: Deflect the opponent's sword towards his right eye as if you were trying to slice his neck, giving the impression of aiming at his nape.

Quick approach with a short sword: If your 'long sword' is rather short, do not hesitate to quickly approach the enemy without seeking to parry, threatening him with your left hand directed towards his face.

So these are the three methods of parrying. Remember that you can always close your left hand and threaten the enemy's face with your fist. Good training is essential to master these techniques.

Aiming at the Face

'Aiming at the Face' means that when you are in confrontation with the enemy, your intention is to threaten his face, following the line of the blades with the tip of your long sword. If you intend to aim at his face, you can then 'mount' his body and face, thus creating various opportunities to prevail. Focus on this technique: when in combat the enemy seems 'mountable', victory can be swift, so do not forget to aim at the face. The value of this technique must be sought through diligent training.

Aiming at the Heart

'Aiming at the Heart' means that during a fight, if there are obstacles above or to the sides or in any context where it is difficult to slash, you should point towards the enemy. You must aim at the enemy's chest without letting the tip of your long sword waver, showing the enemy the back of the blade squarely, with the intention of deflecting his sword. This technique is often useful when we are tired or when, for some reason, our long sword does not slash well. You must understand how to apply this method.

Reprimanding 'Tut-TUT!'

'Reprimanding' means that when the enemy tries to counterattack during your assault, you launch a counterattack from below, as if threatening him, trying to dominate him. With very quick timing, strike while reprimanding the enemy. Push upwards, 'Tut!', and cut 'TUT!'. This timing often repeats during an exchange of blows. To master this technique, you must practice it repeatedly.

The Snapping Parry

The 'Snapping Parry' means that when you cross swords with the enemy, you respond to his assault by striking his sword with a rhythm of tee-dum, tee-dum, snapping against his sword and cutting him. The spirit of this parry is neither to block nor to strike hard, but to strike the enemy's sword in response to his attack, with the primary goal of cutting him quickly. If you understand the timing, your sword tip will not be repelled, even slightly. Conduct thorough research to understand this.

Facing Multiple Enemies

'Facing Multiple Enemies' applies when you are fighting alone against several. Deploy your main and secondary swords and adopt a wide stance. The idea is to make the enemies run from one side to the other, even if they come from all directions. Observe the order of attack and confront those who attack first. Sweep your gaze widely, examining the order of attacks carefully, and alternate strikes left and right with your swords. Do not wait: quickly resume your stance and cut down the enemies as they advance. Regardless of the method, the goal is to group the enemies together, as if they were bound, and as soon as they are grouped, strike powerfully without giving them space to move.

The Advantage in Combat

One can know the way to win through the strategy of the long sword, but this cannot be clearly explained in writing. You must train diligently to understand how to achieve victory.

Oral tradition: 'The true Way of Strategy is revealed in the long sword.

A Single Strike

You can achieve certain victory by adopting the spirit of the 'single strike'. Reaching this state of mind is difficult without a solid understanding of strategy. If you train seriously in this Way, the strategy will emanate naturally from your heart and will allow you to win at will. You must train with diligence.

Direct Communication

The spirit of 'Direct Communication' reflects the way the true Way of the Ni To Ichi school is received and transmitted.

Oral tradition: 'Teach the strategy to your body.'

The above book outlines the major principles of sword fighting according to the Ichi school. To learn to win with the long sword in strategy, start by mastering the five approaches and the five attitudes, and naturally integrate the Way of the long sword into your body. You must understand the spirit and timing, wield the long sword naturally, and harmonize the movements of your body and legs with your spirit. Whether you face one or two opponents, you will then perceive the value of the strategy.

Study the content of this book, approaching each element one after the other. Through fights with enemies, you will gradually come to understand the principle of the Way.

With determination and patience, integrate the virtue of all this, occasionally raising your hand in combat. Maintain this spirit every time you cross swords with an enemy.

Progress step by step on the road of a thousand miles.

Study strategy over the years and achieve the spirit of the warrior. Today's victory over your yesterday's self prefigures tomorrow's victory over lesser men. To defeat more skilled opponents, train according to this book, without letting your heart be distracted. Even if you manage to kill an enemy, if it does not rest on what you have learned, it is not the true Way.

By mastering this Way of victory, you will be able to defeat several dozen men. What matters then is your skill in sword fighting, which you will develop through battles and duels.

THE BOOK OF FIRE

In this 'Book of Fire' of the Ni To Ichi school of strategy, I treat combat as if it were fire.

Firstly, people have a narrow view of the benefits of strategy. Using only their fingertips, they know the advantages of only three out of the five centimeters of the wrist. They let a confrontation be decided, like with a folding fan, simply by the length of their forearms. They specialize in insignificant details like dexterity, learning trivialities such as the movements of hands and legs with the bamboo training sword.

In my strategy, the preparation to defeat enemies is done through numerous confrontations, fighting for survival, discovering the meaning of life and death, learning the Way of the sword, assessing the strength of attacks, and understanding the Way of the 'edge and ridge' of the sword.

Small techniques are not profitable, especially when wearing full armor. My Way of Strategy is the infallible method for winning when fighting for your life, alone against five or ten opponents. There is nothing erroneous in the principle 'one man can beat ten, so a thousand men can beat ten thousand'. You must study this. Of course, you cannot gather a thousand or ten thousand men for daily training. But by training alone with a sword, you can become a master in strategy, understand the enemy's strategy, his strength and resources, and learn to apply strategy to defeat ten thousand enemies.

He who wishes to master the essence of my strategy must study diligently, train morning and evening. Thus, he can perfect his skill, free himself from himself, and realize extraordinary abilities. He will then possess a miraculous power.

This is the practical result of the strategy.

According to the Place

Analyze your environment.

Position yourself so that the sun is at your back. If the situation does not allow it, try at least to have it on your right. In buildings, position yourself with the entrance at your back or on your right. Make sure you are not obstructed at the rear and have free space on your left, your right side being occupied by your lateral stance. At night, if the enemy is visible, keep the fire behind you and the entrance to your right, or adopt a posture similar to the one mentioned earlier. Overlook the enemy and choose slightly elevated positions to fight. For example, the Kamiza in a house is considered a high place.

When the fight starts, always strive to direct the enemy to your left. Push him towards uncomfortable positions, and try to keep him back to these difficult places. When the enemy is in a tricky position, do not give him the chance to look around, but pursue him conscientiously and immobilize him. In houses, push the enemy towards thresholds, lintels, doors, verandas, pillars, etc., without letting him grasp the situation. Always direct the enemy to places where footing is precarious, towards lateral obstacles, etc., exploiting the advantages of the place to establish dominant positions from which to fight. You must study and train diligently in this.

The Three Methods to Forestall the Enemy

The first is to forestall him by attacking. This technique is called Ken No Sen (to overtake him).

Another method is to forestall him as he attacks. This is called Tai No Sen (waiting for the initiative).

The last method applies when you and the enemy attack simultaneously. This method is called Tai Tai No Sen (accompanying and forestalling).

There are no other methods for taking the initiative besides these three. As taking the initiative can allow you to win quickly, it is one of the most important elements of strategy. Taking the initiative involves several things. You must optimize the situation, perceive the enemy's spirit in order to understand his strategy and defeat him. It is impossible to write about this in detail.

The First - Ken No Sen

When you decide to attack, stay calm and rush in quickly, overtaking the enemy. Or you can advance in an apparently strong manner but with a reserved spirit, overtaking him with this reserve.

Another option, advance with as strong a spirit as possible and, when you reach the enemy, move your feet a bit faster than usual, destabilizing and quickly overwhelming him.

Or, with a serene spirit, attack with the feeling of constantly crushing the enemy, from beginning to end. The spirit here is to win in the depths of the enemy. All these techniques are part of Ken No Sen.

The Second - Tai No Sen

When the enemy attacks, remain unperturbed but feign weakness. As the enemy reaches you, move suddenly, indicating that you intend to avoid his attack, then rush in and attack strongly

37

as soon as you see the enemy relax. This is one way to do it.

Or, as the enemy attacks, attack even stronger, taking advantage of the disorder resulting in his timing to win. This principle is Tai No Sen.

The Third - Tai Tai No Sen

When the enemy attacks quickly, you must respond strongly and calmly, aim for his weakness as he approaches, and decisively defeat him. If the enemy attacks calmly, you must observe his movements and, with a light posture, synchronize with his movements as he approaches. Act quickly and strike him firmly. This is Tai Tai No Sen.

What is written here cannot be explicitly detailed with words. You must explore and understand the text. In these three ways of preventing the enemy's attack, you must assess the situation. It is not necessarily about attacking first, but if the enemy attacks, you can lead him. In strategy, you effectively win when you prevent the enemy, so you must train well to achieve this.

Holding Firmly the Pillow

'Holding firmly the pillow' means preventing the enemy from getting up. In strategic confrontations, it is unfavorable to be led by the enemy. You must always be able to lead him. Obviously, the enemy will also think of doing this, but he cannot prevent you if you do not give him the opportunity. In strategy, you must stop the enemy in his attempt to strike, repel his thrust, and counter his grip when he tries to struggle. This represents the meaning of 'holding firmly the pillow'. When you have understood this principle, you will anticipate and suppress what the enemy will try to do in combat. The spirit is to counter his attack, his run, his jump, or his strike by anticipating them.

Crossing at a Ford

'Crossing at a ford' can mean crossing the sea at a strait or navigating a vast sea to a crossing point. This metaphor of 'crossing at a ford' can be applied to many situations in life. It involves undertaking a journey even if your friends stay at the harbor, while knowing the route, the state of your ship, and the favorable conditions of the day. If there is a favorable wind, take advantage of it to sail. If the wind changes near your destination, row without sail for the rest of the journey.

This mindset can be applied to everyday life; always think of 'crossing at a ford'. In strategy, it is also crucial to 'cross at a ford'. Assess the enemy's capabilities, know your own strengths, and cross at the opportune moment, just like a good captain navigates carefully. If you manage to cross at the best place, you can relax. 'Crossing at a ford' means attacking the enemy's weak point and positioning yourself advantageously. This is how to win a large-scale strategy. You must study this spirit of crossing carefully.

Knowing the Opportune Moments

'Knowing the opportune moments' means understanding the disposition of the enemy during combat. Is he in full strength or declining? By observing the state of mind of the enemy troops and occupying the best position, you can determine the disposition of the enemy and move your troops accordingly. You can win the victory through this strategic principle, by fighting from an advantageous position.

In a duel, you need to anticipate the enemy and attack after identifying his school of strategy, assessing his quality, and his strengths and weaknesses. Attack unexpectedly, knowing his rhythm, modulation, and the appropriate timing.

Knowing the opportune moments means that if your skills are high, you can perceive the essence of things. If you master strategy perfectly, you will understand the enemy's intentions and thus have many opportunities to win. Study this carefully.

Crushing the Sword

'Crushing the sword' is a principle frequently used in strategy. First, in large-scale strategy, if the enemy shoots first with bows and guns and then attacks, it is difficult for us to respond if we are busy loading our weapons. The idea is to attack quickly while the enemy is still shooting. You must win by 'crushing' at the moment the enemy attacks.

In single combat, a decisive victory cannot be obtained by cutting, with a 'tee-dum tee-dum' feeling, just after the enemy's long sword attack. We must defeat him at the beginning of his attack, with the intention of crushing him so that he cannot get up and attack again. 'Crushing' does not simply mean trampling. Crush with the body, the spirit, and, of course, cut with the long sword. You must imbue yourself with the spirit that prevents the enemy from attacking a second time. Anticipate in all aspects. Once facing the enemy, do not only think of striking him, but of following through after the attack. Deepen this notion.

Understanding 'Collapse'

Everything can collapse: houses, bodies, and enemies collapse when their rhythm is disrupted. In large-scale strategy, when the enemy begins to collapse, you must pursue him without losing this opportunity. If you do not take advantage of your enemies' collapse, they may recover.

In single combat, the enemy can sometimes lose his rhythm and collapse. If you miss this opportunity, he may recover and no longer be as careless afterwards. Focus on the enemy's collapse, pursue him, and attack in a way that does not let him recover. You must accomplish this with a strong spirit. The enemy must be completely brought down so that he cannot reposition himself. You must understand how to completely bring down the enemy.

Putting Yourself in the Enemy's Place

'Putting yourself in the enemy's place' means projecting yourself into the opponent's position. Generally, one imagines a thief trapped in a house as an entrenched enemy. However, in 'becoming the enemy', one feels that the whole world is against us, with no way out. The one who is trapped is like a pheasant; the one who enters to apprehend them is like a hawk. You must understand this.

In large-scale strategy, people often feel that the enemy is powerful, which makes them cautious. But if you have competent soldiers, a good understanding of strategic principles, and the knowledge necessary to defeat the enemy, there is no reason to worry.

In single combat, you must also put yourself in the enemy's place. If you think: 'Here is a master of strategy who knows all the principles', then you will surely lose. Reflect deeply on this.

Releasing the Four Hands

'Releasing the four hands' applies when you and your enemy adopt the same mindset, unable to resolve the conflict. Abandon this mindset and achieve victory through an alternative approach.

In large-scale strategy, in the presence of a 'four hands' situation, do not give up; after all, it is the human condition. Immediately reject this mindset and win with a technique unexpected to the enemy.

In single combat, if you think you are in a 'four hands' deadlock, you must defeat the enemy by changing your mindset and using a technique appropriate to his situation. You must be capable of making this judgment

Moving the Shadow

'Moving the shadow' is used when you cannot perceive the enemy's intentions. In large-scale strategy, when you cannot determine the enemy's position, feign an imminent and powerful attack to discover his plans. It then becomes easy to defeat him with a different method.

In single combat, if the enemy adopts a stance that masks his intentions, feign an attack. The enemy, believing to perceive your intentions, will react and you can thus exploit him. If you neglect this strategy, you will miss the right moment. Study this carefully.

Mastering a Shadow

'Mastering a shadow' is used when you can see the enemy's intention to attack. In large-scale strategy, if the enemy launches an attack, feign a powerful counter to his technique; this will change his mindset. Then modify your approach and prevent his attack with an unexpected spirit.

In single combat, control the enemy's aggressive intentions with appropriate timing and outpace him. Study this principle well.

Transmitting

There are several phenomena that can be transmitted, such as sleepiness, yawning, and even timing.

In large-scale strategy, when the enemy is restless and seems ready to attack hastily, do not be concerned. Display absolute calmness. The enemy, deceived by your calm, will relax in turn. When you perceive that this calmness has been transmitted to him, launch a powerful attack with an unflappable spirit to defeat him.

In single combat, relax your body and mind, then, seizing the moment when the enemy relaxes, attack vigorously and quickly, taking him by surprise.

This process is similar to 'making someone drunk'. You can also instill in the enemy a spirit of boredom, negligence, or weakness. This deserves careful study.

Unbalancing

Several factors can cause imbalance: danger, difficulties, or surprise, for example.

In large-scale strategy, it is crucial to unbalance the enemy. Attack unexpectedly, and while the enemy's mind is undecided, take advantage of your upper hand to defeat him.

In single combat, start by appearing slow, then suddenly attack with strength. Without giving the enemy time to catch his breath and recover, seize the opportunity to win.

Frightening

Fear is often caused by the unexpected. In large-scale strategy, you can frighten the enemy not only by what you show them but also through shouts, making a small troop appear larger than it is, or threatening their flank without notice. Use the enemy's frightened rhythm to prevail.

In single combat, surprise and frighten the enemy with your body, your sword, or your voice to defeat them.

Immersing

When you are engaged in close combat with the enemy and realize you cannot advance, 'immerse' yourself and merge with the enemy. You can win by applying an appropriate technique while being closely linked to him. Whether in large-scale battles or smaller skirmishes, knowing how to 'immerse' yourself in the enemy can often offer you a decisive victory. Losing this closeness often means losing the opportunity to win. Study this well.

Reaching the Angles

Moving solid things by pushing directly is difficult; it's better to 'reach the angles.'

In large-scale strategy, striking at the angles of enemy forces is advantageous. If the angles are overturned, the morale of the entire troops will also collapse. To defeat the enemy, attack relentlessly once the angles have fallen.

In single combat, once the enemy is weakened, victory becomes easy. Weakening the enemy equates to reaching the 'angles' of his body. It is crucial to master this technique, so deepen your study of it.

Sowing Confusion

This means disorienting the enemy.

In large-scale strategy, use your troops to disorient the enemy on the

44

battlefield. Observe his morale and disturb it: 'Here? There? Like this? Slowly? Quickly?'. Victory is assured when the enemy is caught in a rhythm that disrupts his morale.

In single combat, take every opportunity to disorient the enemy with various techniques. Feign an attack and take advantage of his confusion to easily overcome him.

The Three Shouts

There are three times to shout: before, during, and after. Tailor your shout to the situation. The shout expresses vitality. Shout against the fire, the wind, the waves. It demonstrates energy.

In large-scale strategy, shout as loudly as possible at the beginning. During the fight, the shout is more serious. Shout while attacking, then celebrate your victory with a shout. These are the three shouts.

In single combat, feign an attack while shouting to destabilize the enemy, then attack following your shout. Shout after defeating the enemy to announce victory. This is the principle of shouting before and after. Do not shout at the same time as you brandish your weapon, but during the fight, to find a rhythm.

Mingling

In combat, attack the enemy's strong points and, when they retreat, quickly separate and attack another strong point on the edge of their forces. This strategy is like a winding mountain path.

This is a crucial technique in single combat against multiple opponents. Attack enemies on one side, push them back, then find the right moment to attack other strong points, like on a winding path, assessing the disposition of the enemies.

Crushing

This means regarding the enemy as weak and crushing him.

In large-scale strategy, when the enemy has few men or low morale and is disorganized, crush him totally. Crushing lightly might allow him to recover. Learn to crush forcefully, like in a firm handshake.

In single combat, if the enemy is less skilled, loses his rhythm, or adopts an evasive or defensive posture, crush him immediately without consideration or space to breathe. It is crucial to crush him in one blow. The essential thing is not to let him regain his position, even slightly. Deepen your understanding of this technique.

Mountain-Sea Change

The 'mountain-sea' principle means that it is inadvisable to repeat the same action several times against the enemy. Repeating something twice can sometimes be unavoidable, but avoid a third repetition. If you attack unsuccessfully, repeating the same approach greatly diminishes your chances of success. Change your method if you fail again with a technique already used.

If the enemy expects a powerful and immobile attack like a mountain, attack in a fluid and dynamic manner like the sea, and vice versa. Deepen your understanding of this principle.

Penetrating the Depths

Even if you seem able to win, the enemy's spirit may remain untamed, defeated on the surface but not in depth. With the principle of 'penetrating the depths,' attack the enemy's spirit to its core, demoralize him by rapidly changing your attitude. This happens frequently.

Penetrating the depths involves using the long sword, the body, and the spirit. This cannot be generalized or simplified. Once the enemy is defeated in depth, there is no need to remain combative. If the enemy retains his energy, he is difficult to defeat. Practice penetrating the depths, both in broad strategy and in single combat.

Renewal

'Renewal' applies when you are engaged in combat and a stalemate seems to be reached. Abandon your initial efforts, consider the situation with a fresh mind, and triumph with a new rhythm. Renewal involves changing the mind without changing the circumstances, winning victory with a different technique. Explore this concept in both large-scale strategy and close combat.

Rat's Head, Ox's Neck

'Rat's Head, Ox's Neck' symbolizes the need to alternate between attention to detail (rat's head) and the bigger picture (ox's neck) during a fight. If you and your enemy get lost in minor details, suddenly adopt a broader perspective, and alternate between the two. This philosophy is essential to strategy. It should be integrated into daily life and remain present in both large-scale strategies and individual combat. Delve deeper into this notion.

The Commander Knows His Troops

'The commander knows his troops' is a principle applicable to all aspects of combat in my Way of strategy. Using strategic wisdom, consider the enemy as part of your own troops. By adopting this perspective, you can manipulate him at will and easily dominate him. You take on the role of general, while the enemy becomes your subordinate. You must master this concept.

Releasing the Grip

Releasing the grip involves various states of mind. There is the spirit of triumphing without a sword, and that of holding the long sword without necessarily defeating. These varied methods cannot be easily expressed in writing. Thorough training is essential.

The Rock Body

Once you master the Way of Strategy, your body can suddenly become as impenetrable as a rock, insensitive to all attacks. Your posture is unshakeable. This must be transmitted orally.

The above represents my constant reflections on the Ichi school of swordsmanship, noted spontaneously. This is the first time I write about my technique, and the structure may seem disorganized, the clarity difficult to achieve. This book serves as a spiritual guide for those wishing to learn the Way.

Since my youth, my heart has been drawn to the Way of Strategy, dedicating my life to training and seeking the spiritual attitudes of sword combat. Some focus on theory and technique, but they profoundly lack the true spirit.

Those who study in this way may believe they are training body and spirit, but it takes them away from the true Way, leaving a lasting negative impact. The true Way of Strategy is gradually lost. The true essence of sword fighting is the art of defeating the enemy, nothing more. If you grasp and respect the wisdom of my strategy, victory is assured.

THE BOOK OF WIND

In strategy, it is crucial to understand the Ways of other schools. That is why I have recorded various strategic traditions in this Book of Wind. Without knowledge of other schools, it is difficult to grasp the essence of my Ichi school. Other schools may specialize in force techniques with extra-long swords, others in handling the short sword. Some teach a multitude of techniques, contrasting 'surface' and 'interior'.

I clearly show in this book that all these approaches are erroneous. My Ichi school is different, not aiming to monetize skills. Some focus solely on sword handling, limiting themselves to technical mastery. But is dexterity alone sufficient to win? That is not the essence of the Way. I have listed the unsatisfactory points of other schools in this book, and their in-depth study will allow you to appreciate the advantages of my Ni To Ichi school.

Schools Favoring Extra-Long Swords

Some schools have a preference for extra-long swords. According to my strategy, these schools must be considered weak, because they neglect the fundamental principle of defeating the enemy by all necessary means. These schools rely on the length of the sword, hoping to defeat the enemy from a distance.

It is often said: 'An extra inch offers an advantage', but this is the talk of those who do not understand true strategy. It reveals an inferior strategy and a weak mind to depend on the length of the sword and to fight from a distance without resorting to thoughtful strategy.

These schools may value extra-long swords due to their doctrines, but in practice, it is an irrational choice. Is it not true that one can win even without a long sword? With a long sword, these fighters find it difficult to attack the enemy up close because of the size of their weapon. The latter then becomes a burden, putting its bearer at a disadvantage compared to one who wields a shorter sword.

An old saying goes: 'Large and small go hand in hand.' Therefore, do not completely exclude extra-long swords. What I criticize is the preference given to these long blades. If compared to large-scale strategy, a large army can be likened to a long sword, and a small force to a short sword. Can't small groups fight larger forces? There are many examples of small troops triumphing over large armies.

Your strategy is ineffective if you find yourself in a confined space with only a long sword, or if, in a house, you only possess a short sword. Moreover, not everyone has the same physical strength. In my doctrine, I disapprove of narrow and preconceived thinking. Study this carefully.

The Spirit of the Strong Long Sword in Other Schools

It is inappropriate to speak of strong or weak long swords. If you wield the sword with too much force, your strikes will be crude, and victory will elude you. If you place too much emphasis on the power of your strike, it will be excessively strong and ineffective.

When testing a sword, also avoid striking with too much force. In a fight, do not think of striking hard or striking weakly; think only of defeating the enemy. Focus exclusively on his defeat. Do not rely solely on strength, otherwise your blows will be too powerful and ineffective, often causing your own imbalance. Therefore, the saying 'The strongest hand wins' makes no sense.

In large-scale strategy, if you rely on brute force, a battle between two powerful armies will inevitably be fierce, and this on both sides. Without correct principles, the fight cannot be won.

The spirit of my school is based on victory through strategic wisdom, without being distracted by insignificant details. Study this carefully.

Use of Long Short Swords in Other Schools

Using a long sword and a short sword is not the true way to win.

In the past, 'tachi' and 'katana' respectively referred to long and short swords. Individuals with superior strength can handle a long sword with ease, so it is not justified for them to prefer the short sword. They also use the length of spears and halberds. Some choose a long short sword with the intention of leaping and stabbing the enemy at the moment he is defenseless. This inclination is harmful.

Aiming for the moment when the enemy is vulnerable is an entirely defensive approach, inappropriate when in close combat with the opponent. Moreover, this method with a short sword is ineffective against multiple enemies. Some think they can move freely and slash using a long short sword against multiple adversaries, but they must continually parry and end up being overwhelmed. This approach contradicts the true Way of Strategy.

The sure way to win is to disorient the enemy, forcing him to move, while maintaining a strong and upright posture. This principle also applies to large-scale strategy. The essence of strategy is to invade the enemy in numbers and quickly bring about his downfall. Usually, people learn to counter, dodge, and withdraw, which becomes a habit and allows the enemy to manipulate them easily. The Way of Strategy is direct and sincere. You must control the enemy's movements and subject him to your will.

Other Schools and Their Multiple Long Sword Techniques

Placing too much importance on long sword postures is a flawed reasoning. What is called 'posture' in the world only makes sense when the enemy is absent. This has been true since ancient times, and there should not be a 'modern' way of proceeding in duels. You must force the enemy into uncomfortable positions. Postures are useful in situations where you must remain stationary, like defending castles or arranging troops, showing firmness in the face of assault. In duels, however, you should always be ready to take the initiative and attack. Posture is the spirit of anticipating an attack.

In strategic duels, you must disrupt the opponent's posture. Attack where his mind is relaxed, sow confusion, irritate and frighten him. Take advantage of the enemy's disarray to win. I do not like the defensive spirit called 'posture'. Thus, in my Way, there is a concept named 'Posture-Non-Posture'.

In large-scale strategy, we deploy our troops considering our strength, observing the number of enemies, and analyzing the battlefield. This is the beginning of the battle. The spirit of attacking first is entirely different from that of being attacked. Effectively parrying an attack with a firm attitude and effectively repelling the enemy's assault is similar to creating a wall of spears and halberds. When you attack, your determination should be such that you would be ready to tear stakes from a wall to use as weapons. Examine this carefully.

The Use of Eyes in Other Schools

Some schools advocate fixing your gaze on the enemy's long sword. Others advise focusing on the hands, some on the face, and still others on the feet, etc. If you concentrate your gaze on these points, your mind can be disturbed and your strategy compromised.

I will explain this in detail. Footballers do not constantly fix their gaze on the ball, but with good technique on the field, they can play well. With practice, sight is not the only means of perception. Expert musicians, for example, have the score in front of them, or handle their instruments in different ways, but this does not mean they constantly fix their gaze on them. They see naturally.

In the Way of Strategy, after many battles, you can easily assess the speed and position of the enemy's sword, and by mastering this Way, you will discern the intensity of his spirit. In strategy, to fix the gaze means to probe the heart of man.

On a large scale, the element to watch is the strength of the enemy. There are two methods of seeing: 'perception' and 'vision'.

Perception involves focusing intensely on the enemy's mind, observing the state of the battlefield, and following the progress of the fight. This is the certain way to victory.

In single combat, avoid focusing on details. As mentioned earlier, focusing on details and neglecting the essential will confuse your mind, and victory will escape you. Study this principle well and train diligently.

Use of Feet in Other Schools

There are various ways of using the feet: floating walk, jumping, bouncing, striding, crow steps, and other methods of agile walking. According to my strategy, all of these are unsatisfactory.

I do not favor the floating walk as it tends to make movements too light. You must walk firmly.

I also do not appreciate jumping because it creates an irregular spirit. No matter the extent of the jump, it is not justified.

Bouncing walk engenders an indecisive spirit. The stride is a 'waiting' method which I particularly disapprove of.

Apart from these techniques, there are different methods of rapid walking. Sometimes, you may encounter the enemy on swampy, muddy, rocky terrain, or on narrow paths, where you cannot jump or walk rapidly.

In my strategy, my walking style does not change. I always walk as I would normally. You must never lose control of your feet. Adjust your pace, neither too fast nor too slowly, according to that of the enemy.

This approach is also essential in large-scale strategy. If you attack too quickly without understanding the enemy's spirit, your rhythm will be disturbed. If you advance too slowly, you will not be able to take advantage of the enemy's disorder. You must win by exploiting the weaknesses and disorganizations of the enemy. Train well in this.

Speed in Other Schools

Speed is not intrinsic to the true Way of Strategy. The notion of speed implies that things can seem fast or slow, depending on whether they are in rhythm or not. Regardless of the Way, a master of strategy never appears fast.

Some can walk at a pace of one hundred to one hundred and twenty kilometers a day, but this does not mean they are running continuously from morning to night. Inexperienced runners may give the impression of running all day, but their performance is mediocre.

In the Way of dance, experienced dancers can sing while dancing without any problem. In contrast, beginners who try this slow down and their mind is preoccupied. For example, the melody 'old pine tree' played on a skin drum seems calm, but when a beginner tries to play it, they slow down and their mind is preoccupied. Very skilled people can maintain a fast rhythm, but it is bad to do so hastily. If you try to play too fast, you will lose the rhythm. Of course, being too slow is also bad. Truly gifted people never lose the rhythm, they are always measured and never seem overwhelmed. This example illustrates the principle well.

What is called 'speed' is actually detrimental in the Way of Strategy. The reason is that depending on the terrain - whether it's a marsh, a field, etc. - you may not be able to move your body and legs quickly in sync. You will be even less able to strike quickly if you have a long sword in this situation. If you try to strike quickly, as if you were using a fan or a short sword, you will not succeed in cutting properly. It is important to understand this.

In large-scale strategy too, a quick and restless mind is to be avoided. Your state of mind must be calm and composed, as if you were holding a pillow; thus, you will never be late, not even for a moment.

When your opponent acts in a reckless and hasty manner, you must do the opposite and remain calm. You must not be influenced by your opponent. Train diligently to master this spirit.

'Inside' and 'Outside' in Other Schools

There is no 'inside' or 'outside' in strategy.

Artistic achievements often have deep meanings, secret traditions, associated with notions of 'inside' and 'outside', but in combat, these distinctions do not exist. When I teach my Way, I start with techniques that are easy to understand, simple doctrines. Gradually, according to the student's progress, I strive to explain deeper principles, concepts that are difficult to grasp. However, understanding comes from experience; therefore, I do not speak of 'inside' and 'outside'. If you venture deeply into the mountains, you will eventually find the way out. All Ways have an inside, and showing the way out can sometimes be useful. In strategy, nothing is really hidden or revealed.

That is why I do not like to transmit my Way through written commitments and rules. Depending on the abilities of my students, I teach the direct Way, dispel the bad influences of other schools, and gradually introduce them to the true Way of the warrior, with a spirit of confidence. You must train diligently.

I have outlined the strategies of other schools in the previous sections. I could detail each of them, from the 'surface' to the 'inside', but I have deliberately omitted the names of the schools and their key points, as different branches interpret the doctrines differently. Opinions diverge, hence different interpretations on the same subject. Thus, no single point of view is valid.

I have presented the general tendencies of other schools in nine points. By examining them honestly, one can see that people have a preference for long or short swords and are concerned with strength, whether for major or minor matters.

In my Ichi school of the long sword, there is no 'inside' or 'outside'. The stances do not have hidden meanings. Simply keep your mind sincere to grasp the virtue of strategy.

THE BOOK OF THE VOID

The Way of the Ni To Ichi Strategy is recorded in this Book of the Void. What is called the spirit of the void is where there is nothing. It is beyond human knowledge. The void is actually nothingness. By knowing what exists, one can understand what does not exist, that is, the void.

People see things erroneously and think that what they do not understand must be the void. This is not the true void, it is confusion. In the Way of Strategy too, those who study think that what they do not understand in their art is the void. This is not the true void.

To master the Way of Strategy as a warrior, you must study thoroughly other martial arts and not deviate from the Way of the warrior. Practice day after day, hour after hour, with a serene mind. Polish your heart and your mind, sharpen your perception and your vision. When your mind is perfectly clear, you will perceive the true void.

Until you realize the true Way, whether in Buddhism or in common sense, you may think that things are correct and orderly. However, an objective view, in accordance with the laws of the world, reveals doctrines straying from the true Way. Understand this spirit well, act with rectitude, with the true spirit as the Way. Apply strategy broadly, correctly, and transparently.

You will then begin to think more broadly, considering the void as the Way and the Way as the void.

In the void, there is virtue and no evil. Wisdom, principle, the Way exist, only the spirit is in the void.

Biography

INTRODUCTION

General Overview of Miyamoto Musashi

Miyamoto Musashi, born in 1584 and died in 1645, is an emblematic and legendary figure of feudal Japan, often celebrated as the greatest samurai of all time. Originating from the province of Harima (present-day Hyōgo Prefecture), Musashi was not only an exceptional warrior but also an accomplished artist, writer, and philosopher. As a rōnin (masterless samurai), he dedicated his life to refining his swordsmanship and developing a deep understanding of martial strategy and life philosophy.

His fame is largely built around his exploits in duels, in which he was almost invincible. It is said that he participated in more than sixty duels, never defeated, a feat that greatly contributed to forging his legend. His unique technique, characterized by the use of two swords (Niten Ichi-ryū technique), was revolutionary at the time and remains studied and respected by martial artists worldwide.

Musashi was also a profound thinker, whose reflections have transcended time and cultural boundaries. His most famous work, "The Book of Five Rings" (Go Rin No Sho), is a treatise on strategy, tactics, and philosophy, widely read and cited, considered a timeless guide to achieving success in combat and in life. His teachings continue to inspire and influence people from all walks of life, from martial artists to entrepreneurs, writers to thinkers.

Beyond the battlefield, Musashi was also a talented painter and sculptor, with a pronounced taste for aesthetics and harmony, reflecting the depth of his understanding of life and art. His rich and diverse legacy embodies the essence of bushidō, the "way of the warrior," and continues to fascinate and inspire millions of people around the world.

Historical Context of Musashi's Era

Miyamoto Musashi, born amidst the final tumults of the Sengoku period, traversed a pivotal era in Japanese history that witnessed the transition from constant civil war to a period of stability under the

Tokugawa shogunate. This transition, from the 16th to the 17th century, was marked by political conflicts and power struggles among daimyōs, deeply shaping the context in which Miyamoto grew up and developed both personally and martially.

During the End of the Sengoku Period (1467-1603), Miyamoto was born into an era of deep divisions, where Japan was fragmented among various feuding feudal lords. Born in this period of chaos, Miyamoto was immersed from an early age in an environment where combat skill was essential for survival and highly valued. This atmosphere of incessant wars nourished his interest and devotion to martial arts, pushing him to become one of the most respected and influential warriors of his time.

With the Dawn of the Edo Period (1603-1868), Miyamoto experienced the shift towards a period of political stabilization and relative peace. This new phase ended the civil wars that had devastated the country, but did not diminish the importance of bushidō or the samurais in Japanese society. Miyamoto, living through this transition, continued to refine his swordsmanship, becoming not only a master in his field but also a teacher, influencing future generations with his expertise and philosophy.

The Edo period also witnessed a cultural renewal, with the development of the arts and the enrichment of samurai philosophy. Miyamoto, as an artist and thinker, actively participated in this cultural flourish, contributing to the art and literature of his time. His work and legacy were shaped by and contributed to this period of cultural renaissance, leaving an indelible mark on Japanese culture.

Thus, the life of Miyamoto Musashi unfolds as a living reflection of the transitions, conflicts, and cultural evolutions of his era. From his birth in a time of unending war to his death in a unified and pacified Japan, Miyamoto was not only a witness to these major changes but also played an active role in the cultural and martial fabric of his country, making his legend a timeless symbol of the spirit of an era gone by yet still present in the collective memory of Japan.

YOUTH AND TRAINING

Place and Date of Birth

Miyamoto Musashi was born around 1584, although the exact date remains a topic of debate among historians. The most commonly accepted date is March 12, 1584. He was born in the village of Miyamoto, in the province of Mimasaka (now located in Okayama Prefecture), Japan. This region, known for its rich martial heritage, is nestled in the heart of the country, providing a conducive environment for the growth and development of a young aspiring warrior.

Musashi was born into a family of the samurai (lord) class. His father, Munisai, was an expert in martial arts, renowned for his mastery of the sword and the jutte (a type of baton). Munisai passed on his passion and expertise to his son from an early age, laying the foundations of Musashi's martial education. This early transmission of the samurai code and skills played a decisive role in shaping the young Musashi, who grew up with a deep respect and fascination for martial arts.

Family and Childhood

Indeed, Miyamoto Musashi grew up in a family that was deeply rooted in the tradition of martial arts. His father, Shinmen Munisai, an eminent martial arts practitioner, was a key figure in Musashi's initial training, instilling in him the fundamental principles of martial arts and the way of the warrior from a very young age.

However, Musashi's family life was far from stable or idyllic. His mother died when he was still very young, and his relationship with his father was tense and complicated. At the age of seven, following his parents' separation, Musashi was sent to live with his maternal uncle, a monk named Dorinbo, in a monastery where he received a basic education (reading and writing) and spiritual training.

In the monastery, Musashi not only studied Buddhist sutras but was also introduced to calligraphy and meditation, skills and practices that would accompany him throughout his life. His uncle also played a key role in his initiation into the art of the sword, enriching his martial training.

Musashi was a vigorous and determined child, with a keen interest in martial arts. He showed early signs of martial genius and exceptional independence of spirit. According to legend, he won his first duel at the age of 13 (duels at that time were fights to the death), an early indication of the strength, skill, and determination that would characterize him in adulthood.

The family context and conditions of his childhood deeply influenced Musashi, shaping his character and approach to life and combat. The premature death of his mother, difficult relations with his father, and the strict and disciplined education he received at the monastery all played a role in shaping the young warrior, instilling in him both an indomitable resilience and a deep understanding of martial arts and philosophy.

First Experience

Miyamoto Musashi's first duel, a pivotal moment that marked the beginning of his legend, took place in 1604 when he was just 13 years old. This confrontation occurred near the Hirafuku temple in Mimasaka in present-day Japan. His opponent was Arima Kihei, a practitioner of the traditional Tenshin Shōden Katori Shintō-ryū school of combat.

Musashi, born in a period when Japan was slowly emerging from the chaos of the Sengoku era to enter the more peaceful Edo era, lived in a society where dueling was a common way to resolve disputes and prove one's worth as a warrior. The young Musashi, eager to test and prove his combat skills, challenged Arima Kihei, who was in the region to give a demonstration of his abilities.

The duel was highly formal, with spectators gathered to witness the clash between the young prodigy and the experienced warrior. Musashi, employing a strategy he would perfect throughout his life, arrived late, thereby irritating Arima and gaining a psychological advantage from the start. When the fight began, Musashi, armed with a bokken (wooden sword), quickly implemented his tactical and technical superiority. With bold and unpredictable movements, he managed to unseat Arima, disarming him and ultimately beating him to death. This duel was not only the beginning of Musashi's reputation as an undefeated duelist but also an early demonstration of his combat philosophy, favoring ingenuity, strategy, and a deep understanding of human nature.

This first duel, though brutal in its outcome, established Musashi not only as a leading warrior but also as a figure who would become legendary for his contributions to kenjutsu and martial philosophy. Through this victory and those that followed, Musashi began to weave the legend of a samurai whose life and teachings continue to inspire and influence well beyond martial arts, in many aspects of Japanese culture and thought.

DUETS AND MARTIAL CONQUESTS

Enumeration of Other Duels

Duel Against the Yoshioka School Disciples:
At the age of sixteen, Musashi went to Kyoto, where he faced the three brother disciples of the Yoshioka School, one of the most renowned martial arts schools of the time. He began by challenging Yoshioka Seijuro, the master of the school, and defeated him using a bōken again, deeply humiliating Seijuro and the Yoshioka School. Subsequently, he also faced and defeated Yoshioka Denshichiro and Yoshioka Matashichiro, the other notable figures of the school, thus solidifying his reputation as an invincible swordsman.

Muso Gonnosuke:
Musashi also had a famous duel against Muso Gonnosuke, a renowned master of the long staff (bojutsu). Gonnosuke was a formidable opponent who had studied under several reputable schools. In their first encounter, Musashi disarmed Gonnosuke without killing him. Gonnosuke later returned for a second duel after further perfecting his techniques, but the outcomes of this meeting are subject to debate among historians.

Each of these duels in Musashi's youth played a crucial role in shaping his legend and approach to martial arts. He relied not only on brute strength or technique but also on psychology, intuition, and the environment to his advantage, often anticipating his opponents' moves and responding with disconcerting precision and speed. These early victories laid the foundations for Musashi's illustrious career, making him one of the most famous and respected samurais in Japanese history.

The Notable Duel against Sasaki Kojirō

The duel between Miyamoto Musashi and Sasaki Kojirō is one of the most memorable duels in Miyamoto's martial life. This duel took place in 1612 on the island of Funajima (now called Ganryū-jima) and is one of the most famous and mythologized confrontations in the history of Japanese martial arts. At the time, Sasaki Kojirō was an extremely respected swordsman, known for his "Tsubame Gaeshi" or "Swallow Reversal" technique, a quick and powerful method inspired by the motion of a bird in flight.

Musashi, notorious for his intentionally late arrivals to duels, once again employed this tactic, causing impatience and irritation in Kojirō. When Musashi finally arrived, Kojirō, in fury, attacked with vigor. However, Musashi, who had forged a wooden sword (bokken) from an oar during his journey to the island, parried Kojirō's attacks and eventually delivered a decisive blow to his opponent, ending the duel. The unusually great length of Musashi's improvised weapon is said to have played a crucial role, giving him a reach advantage against Kojirō's long sword (nodachi).

Musashi employed a clever psychological strategy to unbalance Kojirō, exploiting the latter's impatience and anger to prompt him to make mistakes. The use of an improvised weapon, combined with unpredictable and unconventional movements, baffled Kojirō and caused him to lose his advantage.

The duel with Sasaki Kojirō is often cited as one of Musashi's greatest achievements. It not only demonstrated his technical mastery but also his deep understanding of strategy and human psychology in combat. This confrontation has become an integral part of the legend surrounding Musashi, showcasing his ingenuity, calm under pressure, and thoughtful approach to dueling.

The story of this encounter has been told and reinterpreted through the centuries, serving as inspiration in numerous narratives, works of art, and teachings on martial arts, symbolizing the pinnacle of samurai combat.

PERIOD OF WANDERING (MUSHA SHUGYŌ)

Explanation of Musashi's quest for self-improvement

Miyamoto Musashi's life was dedicated to an unceasing quest for self-improvement and mastery in martial arts and beyond. This quest, known in Japanese as "Musha Shugyō," referred to a wandering journey undertaken by warriors in search of training and spiritual enlightenment.

Musashi was never complacent and firmly believed in continuous learning and improvement. He traveled across Japan, engaging in duels, observing other masters, and studying from various martial arts schools. Each experience was an opportunity for him to learn and further perfect his art.

Musashi's quest was not merely a physical journey but also an exercise in introspection and deliberate practice. He devoted countless hours to honing his skills, meditating, and reflecting on the principles of martial arts and the nature of existence.

Throughout his travels and training, Musashi developed his own fencing style, the Niten Ichi-ryū, or the school of two heavens. This unique style, characterized by the simultaneous use of two swords, was the result of his deep reflections and commitment to innovation and excellence. Musashi's adoption of the technique of wielding two swords simultaneously was a remarkable innovation at a time when the norm was the use of a single sword.

Musashi firmly believed that self-mastery was at the heart of mastering martial arts. He invested time in understanding his strengths and weaknesses, his fears and desires, which allowed him to remain calm and focused in the most perilous situations.

Musashi's pursuit of self-improvement was not limited to combat. He was also an artist: an accomplished painter, sculptor, and calligrapher. He saw these artistic disciplines as closely related to the practice of martial arts, with each form of art nourishing and enlightening the others.

The quest for self-improvement was at the heart of Miyamoto Musashi's life and legend. Through an unwavering commitment to learning and improvement, a constant exploration of various forms of art, and deep introspection, Musashi embodies the ideal of the samurai dedicated not only to mastery of combat but also to understanding and self-actualization. His journey, marked by determination and wisdom, continues to inspire and guide individuals across various walks of life.

THE TEACHING & THE NITEN ICHI-RYŪ SCHOOL

The Foundations and Principles of its School

Based on the experiences and reflections of Miyamoto Musashi, the Niten Ichi-ryū school is distinguished by its innovative approach to combat and life philosophy, incorporating fundamental principles derived from the deep wisdom of its founder.

At the heart of this school lies the Nitōken technique, characterized by the simultaneous use of the katana and wakizashi, offering a dynamic combat strategy that allows for attacking and defending at the same time. This method demands perfect harmony and balance between the two hands, symbolizing the quest for balance in martial practice and in life itself.

Musashi emphasized the fluidity of movements and the flexibility of the mind, encouraging adaptability to opponents' strategies to avoid any rigidity. Simplicity, at the core of Niten Ichi-ryū's teaching, promotes direct and effective movements, discarding any superfluous action. The school also places special importance on mental strategy, including understanding the psychology of the opponent and developing concentration and mental clarity.

Continuous learning is a pillar of Musashi's philosophy, which encourages practitioners to engage in constant and thoughtful practice. Finally, Niten Ichi-ryū recognizes the importance of integrating arts, philosophy, and martial arts, illustrating Musashi's conviction that these disciplines are closely linked and mutually enriching.

Miyamoto Musashi's Most Notable Disciples and Their Contributions

Miyamoto Musashi had several disciples who not only inherited his philosophy and techniques but also contributed to perpetuating and further developing the Niten Ichi-ryū school. Here are some of his most notable disciples.

Terao Magonojō:

Terao Magonojō is often considered Musashi's principal disciple. He was the primary recipient of the master's teachings and played a crucial role in transmitting this knowledge to future generations. Magonojō was recognized for his diligent practice and commitment to the art of the sword. His technical mastery and deep understanding of Niten Ichi-ryū's principles allowed him to become a prominent practitioner and teacher.

Terao Kyūmanosuke:

Kyūmanosuke, the younger brother of Magonojō, was also a devoted disciple of Musashi and made significant contributions to the school. He is especially famous for developing and refining certain techniques, thus enriching the technical corpus of Niten Ichi-ryū. Kyūmanosuke actively participated in teaching and spreading

Niten Ichi-ryū's principles, contributing to establishing the school as a respected and influential institution in the martial arts world.

Miyamoto Iori:

As Musashi's adopted grandson, Iori had privileged access to his grandfather's teachings. He faithfully preserved and transmitted Musashi's teachings and techniques, ensuring the school's continuity across generations. Iori also worked to promote Musashi's legacy and memory after his death, making his grandfather a legendary and respected figure in Japanese history.

PERSONAL LIFE

Musashi as an Artist: Painting and Sculpture

In addition to being a renowned warrior, Miyamoto Musashi was also an accomplished artist, expressing his creativity through painting and sculpture. These disciplines allowed him to communicate his philosophy and worldview in a different and complementary way to his martial art.

Painting:

Musashi developed a unique painting style, characterized by simple yet powerful strokes, and a minimalist use of color. His art reflected his life philosophy, with an emphasis on simplicity, clarity, and efficiency.

His works often focused on natural elements and scenes, such as birds, landscapes, or flowers. He found deep inspiration in nature, and used his art to explore and express his connection with the natural world.

His paintings are also imbued with spirituality and philosophy. Through his art, Musashi explored and communicated ideas about life, death, beauty, and transcendence.

Sculpture:

Musashi was also a skilled sculptor, capable of turning wood or stone into delicate and expressive works of art. His sculptures, like his paintings, were often simple but deeply meaningful.

In his sculptures, he frequently chose subjects or symbols laden with philosophical or spiritual meanings, thus creating works that invited reflection and meditation.

Musashi's sculptural works demonstrated a keen sense of harmony and balance, with a particular attention to proportion, form, and texture.

Art and Martial Arts:

For Musashi, art and martial arts were deeply interconnected. He viewed painting and sculpture as extensions of his martial practice, and vice versa. The principles of simplicity, efficiency, and spirituality were present in all his disciplines.

His engagement in the arts was another way to explore and express the "Way" (or "Do" in Japanese). Thus, Musashi's art was not only aesthetically pleasing but also deeply rooted in a quest for understanding and expressing the ultimate reality related to bushido (the Way of the Warrior).

Musashi's View on Life and Mortality

Miyamoto Musashi, through his writings and life itself, conveyed a deep and contemplative view of life and mortality. This perspective was inextricably linked to his practice of martial arts and his ceaseless quest for improvement and wisdom.

Living in an era characterized by conflicts and duels, death was a constant and tangible presence for Musashi. He embraced mortality not as a tragic end, but as an inevitable and natural component of life. Musashi cultivated the mindset of "mushin" or "mind without mind," a state of complete detachment from the fear of death. This profound acceptance of mortality allowed him to act with calm, clarity, and determination in the most perilous situations.

Inspired by the principles of Buddhism, Musashi recognized impermanence as a fundamental characteristic of life. He saw life as a constant flow of changes and transformations, with death as a transition rather than an absolute end.

This awareness of impermanence made him extremely adaptable and resilient in the face of life's uncertainties. He sought to navigate fluidly through situations, embracing change rather than resisting it.

For Musashi, the way of the warrior (or "Bushido") was a quest for deep meaning and personal fulfillment. He aspired to live a life that reflected principles of courage, honor, and self-discipline, integrating these values into every action and decision. His values were dictated by the principles of bushido.

Well aware of physical mortality, Musashi believed in a form of immortality through artistic, philosophical, and martial contributions. His work, "The Book of Five Rings," as well as his paintings and sculptures, are testimonies to this aspiration to leave a lasting legacy.

LATER YEARS AND DEATH

Gradual Retreat from Public Life

In the last years of his life, Miyamoto Musashi gradually withdrew from the public scene and the world of competitive martial arts. This withdrawal was a time of deep reflection, writing, and passing on his knowledge to his disciples.

Musashi progressively ceased to participate in duels and fights. This reflected not only his advancing age but also a change in his perspective on martial arts and life.

With the withdrawal from active dueling, he devoted more time to teaching and imparting his techniques and philosophy to his disciples and other aspiring warriors.

During this period of withdrawal, Musashi wrote "The Book of Five Rings" ("Go Rin no Sho"), a masterful work that condenses his thoughts and teachings on strategy, tactics, and the philosophy of martial arts. He also wrote a list of the 21 principles of bushido (the Way of the Warrior), called "Dokkodo."

These years were also marked by deep meditation and introspection, as he explored and solidified his understanding of the way of the warrior and the transient nature of life.

Musashi immersed himself in his artistic practices, producing a series of paintings and sculptures that reflected his state of mind and worldview.

Retired, he also spent a lot of time in nature, finding inspiration and tranquility in the mountainous and forested landscapes of Japan.

Musashi dedicated his last years to guiding and advising his closest disciples, ensuring that his teachings and philosophy would endure after his death.

As a warrior who had often brushed with death, Musashi approached his mortality with deep serenity and acceptance, imparting to his students not only the art of combat but also the art of living and dying with dignity and honor.

Miyamoto Musashi's gradual withdrawal from public life was not a passive seclusion but rather a deliberate space for contemplation, artistic expression, and the transmission of wisdom. This critical period of his life ensured that his legacy, encapsulated in his writings, artworks, and students, would continue to inspire and influence future generations long after his departure.

Circumstances and Location of His Death

Miyamoto Musashi, after leading a life full of adventures, challenges, and profound reflections, passed away in circumstances that reflect the serenity and self-mastery he had cultivated throughout his life.

Musashi retired to the Reigandō cave, a secluded and peaceful place, in his final moments. This location offered a tranquil environment, ideal for meditation and deep reflection.

According to historical documents, his death was peaceful, occurring during the night. It is said that he passed away sitting in the zazen position, a meditation posture, which demonstrates his peace of mind and conscious preparation to leave this world.

Miyamoto Musashi died on May 19, 1645. His last days were devoted to writing, meditating, and passing on his knowledge to his closest disciples.

The Reigandō cave, located in Kumamoto, Japan, is the place of his death. The cave is near the Myōhōin temple, a place surrounded by nature, with mountains and forests providing a solemn and beautiful setting.

Today, this place has become a memorial site and a meditation space for visitors, where they can pay homage to Musashi's life and legacy. The death of Miyamoto Musashi was in keeping with his life: marked by dignity, self-control, and deep spirituality. The place of his death, Reigandō, remains a space where the echo of his wisdom and the indelible trace of his indomitable and contemplative spirit still resonate today.

BIBLIOGRAPHY AND SOURCES

Main Works:
'Miyamoto Musashi: His Life and Writings' by Kenji Tokitsu:
Tokitsu offers a detailed analysis of Musashi's life, his writings, and his legacy within the Japanese historical and cultural context.

'The Lone Samurai: The Life of Miyamoto Musashi' by William Scott Wilson:
A comprehensive biography that explores Musashi's life, duels, and philosophy, based on extensive research and historical sources.

Academic Articles:
'Miyamoto Musashi – Examination of a Legend' in 'Journal of Asian Martial Arts':
This academic article explores the legend of Musashi, separating myth from reality and examining the impact of his life on Japanese culture.

'Musashi's Dokkodo (The Way of Walking Alone): Half Crazy, Half Genius – Finding Modern Meaning in the Sword Saint's Last Words':
An analysis of Musashi's final thoughts and teachings, focusing on their relevance and application to modern life.

Historical Documents:

'Niten Ki (Chronicles of Niten)':
A historical document providing a contemporary account of Musashi's life, duels, and teachings.

Online Resources:
Online encyclopedias and databases on martial arts:
For specific information on techniques, martial arts schools, and historical figures associated with Musashi.

Others:
Exhibition catalogs of Miyamoto Musashi's artwork:
These catalogs provide analyses of his artwork, offering a deeper understanding of his talent and artistic vision.

The book of five rings

Made in the USA
Coppell, TX
31 July 2024

35399374R00062